QUICK & EASY
WOK
COOKBOOK

Consultant Editor:
Valerie Ferguson

southwater

Contents

Introduction

Stir-frying in a wok is an ancient cooking technique which originated in the Far East. It has now become popular the world over, and this is not surprising: food that has been stir-fried in the correct way is healthy, delicious and highly convenient. The unique shape of the wok allows ingredients to be cooked speedily at a high temperature in very little fat, thus retaining maximum flavour and nutrients. A wok can also be used for steaming and deep frying. It is therefore ideal for both quick, nourishing, everyday one-pot meals and impromptu entertaining.

Many of the recipes in this book are Oriental favourites, originating from all over the Far East, but traditional Western dishes have been adapted to take advantage of this cooking method – you will find recipes for Sukiyaki-style Beef and Prawn Fu-yung as well as Stir-fried Pork with Mustard and Chicken Liver Stir-fry.

Once you begin, you will be amazed at the versatility of wok cooking and may find that you can adapt some of your own favourite dishes. Don't be afraid to experiment. Whether you want a spicy starter or a main course bursting with flavour, your wok can provide it.

Equipment

Most of the cooking equipment you already have will produce good results, but if you would like to invest in some authentic tools of the trade, the following may be of interest:

Bamboo Skewers
These are widely used for barbecues and grilled foods.

Chopping Board
A good-quality chopping board with a thick surface will last for years.

Chopping Knife
If you are not comfortable using a cleaver, a large, heavy chopping knife can be used.

Citrus Zester
This tool is designed to remove the zest of the fruit while leaving the bitter white pith.

Cleaver
The weight of the cleaver makes it ideal for chopping all kinds of ingredients. Keep the blade sharp.

Cooking Chopsticks
These are extra long and allow you to stir ingredients safely in the wok.

Draining Wire
Used mainly for deep frying, this is designed to sit on the side of the wok.

Food Processor
This is a quick alternative to the pestle and mortar.

Ladle
A long-handled ladle is very useful for spooning out soups, stock or sauces.

Pestle & Mortar
These are useful for grinding small amounts of spices.

Rice Paddle
This is used to lightly fluff up rice after cooking.

Saucepan
A good saucepan with a tight-fitting lid is essential for cooking rice.

Sharpening Stone
A traditional tool for sharpening knives and cleavers, available from hardware stores.

Stainless-steel Skimmer
This can be used when strong flavours are likely to affect bare-metal cooking implements.

Wire Skimmer
This is used to remove cooked food from boiling water or hot fat.

Wok
The shape of the wok, with its deep, sloping sides, allows ingredients to be cooked in a minimum of fat, thus

retaining freshness and flavour. This shape also makes it suitable for deep frying, braising and steaming. There are several varieties available including the carbon-steel, round-bottomed wok or Pau wok, best suited to a gas hob. The carbon-steel, flat-bottomed wok is best for use on electric or solid-fuel hobs, as it will give a better distribution of heat.

Woks have one or two handles; select wooden-covered handles, if possible. A metal domed lid is essential for steaming or braising.

A selection of equipment to make wok cooking simpler:
1 wok and lid; 2 saucepan; 3 bamboo skewers; 4 food processor; 5 cooking chopsticks; 6 draining wire; 7 citrus zester; 8 sharpening stone; 9 chopping board; 10 chopping knife; 11 ladle; 12 wok spatula; 13 stainless-steel skimmer; 14 pestle and mortar; 15 rice paddle; 16 cleavers; 17 wire skimmer.

Techniques

Seasoning Your Wok

If you are using a new wok, which is not non-stick, you will need to prepare it as follows to ensure the best results and a good non-stick surface.

1 Wash the wok in hot, soapy water to remove traces of the manufacturing process. Rinse and dry.

2 Heat the wok with 30–45 ml/ 2–3 tbsp salt for about 15 minutes, stirring so that the whole surface is coated with the salt. Wipe out the salt and continue to use as recommended.

3 After use, thoroughly wipe out the wok with kitchen paper. A little groundnut oil can be wiped around the inside before storing it away.

Cleaning a Non-stick Wok

To clean a non-stick wok after using, allow the wok to cool slightly, then wipe out the inside with kitchen paper. Where possible, keep washing with detergent to a minimum as this removes the non-stick surface from your wok.

Preparing Fresh Root Ginger

Remove the tough skin with a peeler or a small, sharp knife. Then cut the root into thin strips. Place each piece flat on a chopping board, cut into fine strips and use, or turn the strips around and chop them finely. Always wash your hands thoroughly after preparation.

Preparing Garlic

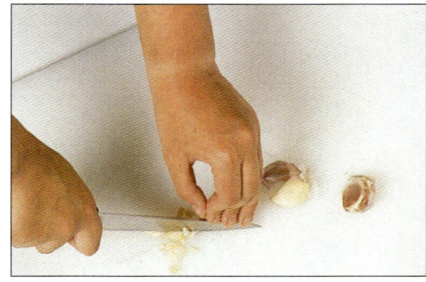

1 Break the garlic clove off the bulb and remove the papery skin. Finely chop the clove, then sprinkle with a little salt and work this in, using the flat side of a knife blade until the garlic softens.

2 Peeled garlic can also be crushed using a garlic press.

General Rules for Stir-frying

Stir-frying takes very little cooking time: often only minutes. For this reason it is important that all the ingredients are prepared ahead of time and cut to the same shape and size. Many recipes require the vegetables to be cut into matchsticks. Stir-frying ensures they will be cooked evenly, retaining crispness and colour.

Beansprouts and Chinese leaves need the minimum of cooking and are added towards the end of cooking time.

1 Always preheat the wok for a few minutes. If adding oil, swirl it into the wok and allow it to heat up before adding the food to be cooked.

2 When adding the first ingredients, reduce the heat a little to ensure they are not overcooked or burnt.

3 Once all the ingredients have been added, quickly increase the heat. This allows them to retain a crisp, fresh texture, and prevents sogginess.

4 Use a long-handled ladle or spatula to keep the ingredients turning as you stir-fry them. This will enable the ingredients to cook as evenly and rapidly as possible.

5 It may be easier to slice any meat that is to be used for stir-frying thinly if it has been frozen slightly for an hour or so beforehand. By the time you have sliced it, the meat will be sufficiently thawed for it to be cooked in the usual way.

Butterfly Prawns

Use raw prawns if you can because the flavour will be better. If you substitute cooked prawns, cut down the stir-fry cooking time by one-third.

Serves 4

INGREDIENTS
350 g/12 oz raw prawns,
   thawed if frozen
50 g/2 oz/½ cup raw peanuts,
   roughly chopped
45 ml/3 tbsp vegetable oil
2.5 cm/1 in piece fresh root ginger,
   peeled and finely chopped
1 garlic clove, crushed
1 fresh red chilli, seeded and
   finely chopped
45 ml/3 tbsp smooth peanut butter
15 ml/1 tbsp chopped
   fresh coriander
fresh coriander sprigs, to garnish

FOR THE DRESSING
150 ml/¼ pint/⅔ cup plain yogurt
5 cm/2 in piece cucumber, diced
salt and freshly ground black pepper

1 To make the dressing, mix together the yogurt, cucumber and seasoning in a bowl, then chill.

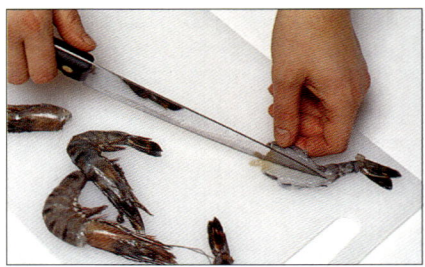

2 Prepare the prawns by removing the heads and shells, leaving the tails intact. Using a small, sharp knife, make a slit along the back of each prawn and remove the black vein, then slit the prawn completely down the back and open it out to make a "butterfly".

3 Heat a wok and dry fry the peanuts, stirring constantly until golden brown. Remove and set aside to cool. Wipe out the wok with kitchen paper.

4 Reheat the wok, add the oil and, when hot, add the ginger, garlic and chilli. Stir-fry for 1-2 minutes until the garlic is softened but not brown.

5 Add the prawns, then increase the heat and stir-fry for 1–2 minutes until they turn pink. Stir in the peanut butter and stir-fry for 2 minutes.

6 Add the chopped coriander, then scatter in the peanuts. Garnish with coriander sprigs and serve with the cucumber dressing.

Mussels in Black Bean Sauce

Buy cooked mussels on the half-shell for this delicious dish.

Serves 4

INGREDIENTS
15 ml/1 tbsp vegetable oil
2.5 cm/1 in piece fresh
   root ginger, peeled and
   finely chopped
2 garlic cloves, finely chopped
1 fresh red chilli, seeded
   and chopped
15 ml/1 tbsp black bean sauce
15 ml/1 tbsp dry sherry
5 ml/1 tsp caster sugar
5 ml/1 tsp sesame oil
10 ml/2 tsp dark soy sauce
20 cooked New Zealand
   green-shelled mussels
2 spring onions, 1 shredded and 1 cut into
   fine rings

2 Have ready a wok with about 5 cm/2 in of boiling water and a bamboo steamer that will rest neatly over it. Place the mussels in a single layer on a heatproof plate. Spoon over the sauce.

3 Sprinkle the spring onion rings over the mussels and place the plate in the steamer. Steam over a high heat for about 10 minutes or until the mussels have heated through. Serve garnished with shredded spring onions.

1 Heat the vegetable oil in a small frying pan. Fry the ginger, garlic and chilli with the black bean sauce for a few seconds, then add the sherry and caster sugar and cook for 30 seconds more. Remove from the heat and stir in the sesame oil and soy sauce.

VARIATION: Large scallops in their shells can be cooked in the same way. Do not overcook the shellfish.

Crisp-fried Crab Claws

A chilli dip provides a spicy contrast to the sweet crab meat.

Serves 4

INGREDIENTS

50 g/2 oz/½ cup rice flour
15 ml/1 tbsp cornflour
2.5 ml/½ tsp granulated sugar
1 egg
60 ml/4 tbsp cold water
1 lemon grass stalk,
    finely chopped
2 garlic cloves, finely chopped
15 ml/1 tbsp chopped
    fresh coriander
1–2 fresh red chillies, seeded
    and chopped
5 ml/1 tsp fish sauce
oil, for deep frying
12 half-shelled crab claws
freshly ground black pepper

FOR THE CHILLI VINEGAR DIP

45 ml/3 tbsp sugar
120 ml/4 fl oz/½ cup water
120 ml/4 fl oz/½ cup red
    wine vinegar
15 ml/1 tbsp fish sauce
2–4 fresh red chillies, seeded
    and chopped

1 To make the chilli vinegar dip, put the sugar and water in a saucepan and bring to the boil, stirring until the sugar dissolves. Lower the heat and simmer for 5–7 minutes. Stir in the wine vinegar, fish sauce and chillies to taste. Set aside.

2 Combine the rice flour, cornflour and sugar in a bowl. Beat the egg with the cold water in a small bowl. Add the egg mixture to the flour mixture and stir well to form a light batter.

3 Add the lemon grass, garlic, coriander, red chillies, fish sauce and black pepper. Stir to mix thoroughly.

4 Heat the oil in a wok. Pat dry the crab claws with kitchen paper and dip one at a time in the batter.

5 Gently drop the battered claws into the hot oil, a few at a time. Fry until golden brown, then drain on kitchen paper and keep warm.

6 Pour the chilli vinegar dip into a serving bowl. Serve the fried crab claws hot on a large, warmed platter or on individual plates, accompanied by the dip.

COOK'S TIP: To check whether the oil is hot enough before adding the crab claws, drop in a cube of bread. If it browns within 1 minute, the oil is ready.

Chicken Liver Stir-fry

The final sprinkling of lemon, parsley and garlic gives this dish a delightfully fresh flavour and wonderful aroma. Serve with white toast.

Serves 6

INGREDIENTS
500 g/1¼ lb chicken livers
75 g/3 oz/6 tbsp butter
175 g/6 oz field mushrooms
50 g/2 oz chanterelle mushrooms
3 garlic cloves, finely chopped
2 shallots, finely chopped
150 ml/¼ pint/⅔ cup medium sherry
3 fresh rosemary sprigs
30 ml/2 tbsp chopped fresh parsley, plus
    extra, to garnish
grated rind of 1 lemon
salt and freshly ground
    black pepper

1 Clean and trim the chicken livers to remove any gristle or muscle. Season the livers generously with salt and pepper.

2 Heat a wok and add 15 g/½ oz/ 1 tbsp of the butter. When it has melted, add the livers in batches (melting more butter where necessary, but reserving 25 g/1 oz/2 tbsp for the vegetables), and flash-fry until golden brown. Drain with a slotted spoon, transfer to a plate and keep warm.

3 Cut the field mushrooms into thick slices. Depending on their size, cut the chanterelles in half.

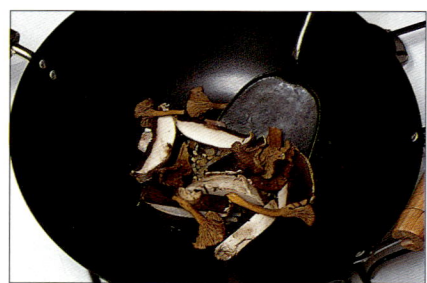

4 Reheat the wok and add the remaining butter. When it has melted, stir in two-thirds of the chopped garlic and the shallots and stir-fry for 1 minute, stirring continuously, until golden brown. Stir in the mushrooms and continue to cook for a further 2 minutes.

5 Add the sherry, and simmer for 2–3 minutes until syrupy. Add the rosemary, season, and return the livers to the pan. Stir-fry for 1 minute.

6 Serve sprinkled with parsley, lemon rind and the remaining chopped garlic.

Indonesian-style Satay Chicken

Succulent skewered chicken served with a sauce in which the flavours of coconut, peanuts and chilli mingle to surprise the taste buds. This dish would make an unusual start to a dinner party.

Serves 8

INGREDIENTS

50 g/2 oz/½ cup raw peanuts
45 ml/3 tbsp vegetable oil
1 small onion, finely chopped
2.5 cm/1 in piece fresh root ginger, peeled
   and finely chopped
1 garlic clove, crushed
675 g/1½ lb boneless chicken thighs,
   skinned and cut into cubes
90 g/3½ oz creamed coconut,
   roughly chopped
15 ml/1 tbsp chilli sauce
60 ml/4 tbsp crunchy
   peanut butter
5 ml/1 tsp soft dark
   brown sugar
150 ml/¼ pint/⅔ cup milk
1.5 ml/¼ tsp salt

1 Shell and rub the skins from the peanuts, then soak them in enough water to cover, for 1 minute. Drain the nuts and cut them into slivers.

2 Heat a wok and add 5 ml/1 tsp of the oil. Stir-fry the peanuts for 1 minute until crisp and golden. Remove from the wok with a slotted spoon and drain on kitchen paper.

3 Add the remaining oil to the hot wok. When the oil is hot, add the onion, ginger and garlic and stir-fry for 2–3 minutes until softened but not browned.

4 Add the chicken pieces to the wok and stir-fry for 3–4 minutes until crisp and golden on all sides and cooked through. Remove the chicken pieces from the wok with a slotted spoon, thread on to bamboo skewers and keep warm.

5 Add the creamed coconut to the hot wok in small pieces and stir-fry until melted. Add the chilli sauce and the crunchy peanut butter and simmer gently for 2 minutes. Stir in the sugar, milk and salt, and simmer for a further 3 minutes.

6 Pour the sauce into a serving bowl and sprinkle with the peanuts. Hand round the sauce as an accompaniment to the skewered chicken.

Braised Fish Fillet

White fish in a tasty sauce.

Serves 4

INGREDIENTS
450 g/1 lb fillets of lemon sole or plaice,
  cut into bite-size pieces
5 ml/1 tsp salt
½ egg white
30 ml/2 tbsp cornflour, mixed to a thin paste
  with water
vegetable oil, for deep frying
15 ml/1 tbsp finely chopped spring onions
2.5 ml/½ tsp finely chopped fresh root ginger
115 g/4 oz/1½ cups mushrooms, thinly sliced
5 ml/1 tsp soft light brown sugar
15 ml/1 tbsp light soy sauce
30 ml/2 tbsp Chinese rice wine or dry sherry
15 ml/1 tbsp brandy
120 ml/4 fl oz/½ cup water
few drops of sesame oil

1 Mix the fish with a little salt, the egg white and about half of the cornflour paste. Heat the oil in a wok until medium-hot and fry the fish in batches for 1 minute. Drain. Pour off the oil, leaving about 30 ml/2 tbsp.

2 Stir-fry the spring onions, ginger and mushrooms for 1 minute. Add the next five ingredients and bring to the boil. Add the fish, simmer for 1 minute, then thicken with the remaining cornflour paste. Serve, sprinkled with the sesame oil.

Prawn Fu-yung

A delicious and simple dish.

Serves 4

INGREDIENTS
3 eggs, beaten, reserving 5 ml/1 tsp
  egg white
5 ml/1 tsp salt
15 ml/1 tbsp finely chopped spring onions
45–60 ml/3–4 tbsp vegetable oil
225 g/8 oz raw prawns, peeled and deveined
10 ml/2 tsp cornflour, mixed to a thin paste
  with water
175 g/6 oz/1½ cups peas
15 ml/1 tbsp Chinese rice wine or dry sherry

1 Beat the eggs with a pinch of the salt and a pinch of the spring onion. In a wok, scramble the eggs in a little oil over moderate heat. Remove from the wok and reserve.

2 Mix the prawns with a little salt, 5 ml/1 tsp egg white and the cornflour paste. Stir-fry the peas in the remaining hot oil for 30 seconds. Add the prawns and the spring onions and stir-fry for another minute.

3 Stir the scrambled egg into the prawn mixture with a little salt and the wine or sherry. Carefully blend the Fu-yung well and serve.

Right: Braised Fish Fillet (top);
Prawn Fu-yung

Gingered Seafood Stir-fry

A refreshing summer supper, served with plenty of crusty bread to mop up the juices and a glass of chilled dry white wine.

Serves 2

INGREDIENTS
15 ml/1 tbsp sunflower oil
5 ml/1 tsp sesame oil
2.5 cm/1 in piece fresh root ginger, peeled
    and finely chopped
1 bunch spring onions, sliced
1 red pepper, seeded
    and chopped
115 g/4 oz small "queen" scallops
8 large raw prawns, peeled and deveined
115 g/4 oz squid rings
15 ml/1 tbsp lime juice
15 ml/1 tbsp light soy sauce
60 ml/4 tbsp coconut milk
salt and freshly ground
    black pepper
mixed salad leaves,
    to serve

2 Add the scallops, prawns and squid rings and stir-fry over a medium heat for about 3 minutes until the seafood is just cooked.

3 Stir in the lime juice, soy sauce and coconut milk. Simmer, uncovered, for 2 minutes until the juices begin to thicken slightly.

4 Season well. Arrange the mixed salad leaves on serving plates and spoon over the seafood mixture with the juices.

1 Heat the oils in a wok and cook the ginger and spring onions for 2–3 minutes or until golden. Stir in the red pepper and cook for a further 3 minutes.

Green Seafood Curry

This curry is based on a Thai classic. The lovely green colour is imparted by the finely chopped chilli and fresh herbs added during the last few moments of cooking.

Serves 4

INGREDIENTS
225 g/8 oz small ready-prepared squid
225 g/8 oz raw tiger prawns
400 ml/14 fl oz/1⅔ cups
    coconut milk
30 ml/2 tbsp ready-made green
    curry paste
2 fresh kaffir lime leaves,
    finely shredded
30 ml/2 tbsp Thai fish sauce
450 g/1 lb firm white fish fillets, skinned,
    boned and cut into chunks
2 fresh green chillies, seeded and
    finely chopped
30 ml/2 tbsp torn fresh basil or
    coriander leaves
squeeze of lime juice
Thai jasmine rice, to serve

1 Rinse the prepared squid and pat them dry with kitchen paper. Cut the bodies into rings and halve the tentacles, if necessary.

2 Heat a wok until hot, add the prawns and stir-fry without any oil for about 4 minutes until they turn pink.

VARIATION: If you like more fiery curries, increase the amount of green curry paste used.

3 Remove the prawns from the wok and, when they are cool enough to handle, remove the heads and shells. Using a small, sharp knife, make a slit along the back of each one and remove the black vein.

4 Pour the coconut milk into the wok, then bring to the boil, stirring. Add the curry paste, shredded lime leaves and fish sauce. Reduce the heat to a simmer and cook for about 10 minutes to allow the flavours to develop fully.

5 Add the squid, prawns and white fish and cook for 2 minutes. Take care not to overcook the squid as it will become tough very quickly.

6 Stir in the chillies and basil or coriander. Taste and add a squeeze of lime juice. Serve immediately with Thai jasmine rice.

Spiced Prawns with Coconut

Serves 3–4

INGREDIENTS
2–3 fresh red chillies, seeded and chopped
3 shallots, chopped
1 lemon grass stalk, chopped
2 garlic cloves, chopped
thin sliver of dried shrimp paste
2.5 ml/½ tsp ground galangal
5 ml/1 tsp ground turmeric
5 ml/1 tsp ground coriander
15 ml/1 tbsp groundnut oil
250 ml/8 fl oz/1 cup water
2 fresh kaffir lime leaves
5 ml/1 tsp soft light brown sugar
2 tomatoes, peeled, seeded and chopped
250 ml/8 fl oz/1 cup coconut milk
675 g/1½ lb large raw prawns, peeled
  and deveined
squeeze of lemon juice
salt
shredded spring onions and toasted flaked
  coconut, to garnish

1 Using a pestle and mortar, pound the chillies, shallots, lemon grass, garlic, shrimp paste, galangal, turmeric and coriander to form a paste.

2 Heat the wok until hot, add the oil and swirl it around. Add the spice paste and stir-fry for about 2 minutes. Pour in the water and add the kaffir lime leaves, sugar and tomatoes. Simmer for 8–10 minutes until most of the liquid has evaporated.

3 Add the coconut milk and prawns, and cook gently, stirring, for about 4 minutes until the prawns are pink. Taste and adjust the seasoning with salt and a squeeze of lemon juice. Serve at once, garnished with shredded spring onions and toasted flaked coconut.

Squid in a Black Bean Sauce

Salted black beans add a traditionally Chinese flavour to this tasty stir-fry.

Serves 4

INGREDIENTS
30 ml/2 tbsp salted black beans
30 ml/2 tbsp medium-dry sherry
15 ml/1 tbsp light soy sauce
5 ml/1 tsp cornflour
2.5 ml/½ tsp sugar
30 ml/2 tbsp water
45 ml/3 tbsp groundnut oil
450 g/1 lb ready-prepared squid, scored and
    cut into thick strips
5 ml/1 tsp finely chopped fresh root ginger
1 garlic clove, finely chopped
1 fresh green chilli, seeded and sliced
6–8 spring onions, cut diagonally into
    2.5 cm/1 in lengths
½ red and ½ green pepper, seeded and cut
    into 2.5 cm/1 in diamonds
75 g/3 oz shiitake mushrooms, thickly sliced

1 Rinse and finely chop the black beans. Place them in a bowl with the sherry, soy sauce, cornflour, sugar and water. Mix well.

2 Heat a wok until hot, add the oil and swirl it around. When the oil is very hot, add the squid and stir-fry for 1–1½ minutes until opaque and curled at the edges. Remove with a slotted spoon and set aside.

3 Add the ginger, garlic and chilli to the wok and stir-fry for a few seconds. Add the spring onions, peppers and mushrooms, then stir-fry for 2 minutes.

4 Return the squid to the wok and add the sauce. Cook, stirring, for about 1 minute until thickened. Serve at once.

Spicy Chicken Stir-fry

The chicken is marinated in an aromatic blend of spices and then stir-fried with crisp vegetables. If you find it too spicy, serve with a spoonful of soured cream or yogurt. It's just as delicious hot or cold.

Serves 4

INGREDIENTS

2.5 ml/½ tsp ground turmeric
2.5 ml/½ tsp ground ginger
5 ml/1 tsp salt
5 ml/1 tsp freshly ground
   black pepper
10 ml/2 tsp ground cumin
15 ml/1 tbsp ground coriander
15 ml/1 tbsp caster sugar
450 g/1 lb boneless skinless
   chicken breast
1 bunch spring onions
4 celery sticks
2 red peppers, seeded
1 yellow pepper, seeded
175 g/6 oz courgettes
175 g/6 oz mangetouts or
   sugar snap peas
45–60 ml/3–4 tbsp sunflower oil
15 ml/1 tbsp lime juice
15 ml/1 tbsp clear honey

1 Mix together the turmeric, ginger, salt, pepper, cumin, coriander and sugar in a bowl until well combined.

2 Cut the chicken into bite-size strips. Add to the spice mixture and stir to coat the chicken pieces thoroughly. Set aside.

3 Prepare the vegetables. Cut the spring onions, celery and peppers into 5 cm/2 in long, thin strips. Cut the courgettes at a slight angle into thin rounds and top and tail the mangetouts or sugar snap peas.

4 Heat 30 ml/2 tbsp of the oil in a wok. Stir-fry the chicken in batches until cooked through and golden brown, adding more oil if necessary. Remove from the pan and keep warm. Add a little more oil to the pan and cook the spring onions, celery, peppers and courgettes over a medium heat for 8–10 minutes.

5 Add the mangetouts or sugar snap peas and cook for a further 2 minutes.

6 Return the chicken to the pan, with the lime juice and honey. Cook for 2 minutes. Adjust the seasoning and serve.

Sweet-&-sour Chicken Stir-fry

Serves 4

INGREDIENTS
275 g/10 oz Chinese egg noodles
115 g/4 oz sugar snap peas
30 ml/2 tbsp vegetable oil
3 spring onions, chopped
1 garlic clove, crushed
2.5 cm/1 in piece fresh root ginger, peeled
  and grated
5 ml/1 tsp hot paprika
5 ml/1 tsp ground coriander
3 boneless skinless chicken breasts, sliced
115 g/4 oz baby sweetcorn, halved
225 g/8 oz/1 cup beansprouts
15 ml/1 tbsp cornflour
45ml/3 tbsp soy sauce
45 ml/3 tbsp lemon juice
15 ml/1 tbsp sugar
45 ml/3 tbsp chopped fresh coriander or
  spring onion tops, to garnish

1 Bring a large saucepan of salted water to the boil. Add the egg noodles and cook according to the packet instructions. Drain, cover and keep warm in a bowl set over a pan of barely simmering water.

2 Top and tail the sugar snap peas. Heat the oil in a wok. Add the spring onions and cook over a gentle heat. Mix in the next five ingredients, then stir-fry for 3–4 minutes. Add the peas, sweetcorn and beansprouts and steam briefly. Add the noodles.

3 Combine the cornflour, soy sauce, lemon juice and sugar in a small bowl. Add to the wok and simmer briefly to thicken. Serve garnished with chopped fresh coriander or spring onion tops.

Stir-fried Chicken with Basil & Chillies

The unique, pungent flavour of Thai basil gives a special lift to this dish.

Serves 4–6

INGREDIENTS
45 ml/3 tbsp vegetable oil
4 garlic cloves, sliced
2–4 fresh red chillies, seeded and chopped
450 g/1 lb chicken, cut into bite-size pieces
30–45 ml/2–3 tbsp fish sauce
10 ml/2 tsp dark soy sauce
5 ml/1 tsp sugar
10–12 fresh Thai basil leaves

FOR THE GARNISH
2 red chillies, finely sliced, to garnish
20 fresh Thai basil leaves,
    deep fried (optional)

1 Heat the oil in a wok and swirl it around. Add the sliced garlic and chopped chillies and stir-fry until golden.

2 Add the chicken pieces and stir-fry until they change colour. Season with fish sauce, dark soy sauce and sugar. Continue to stir-fry for about 3–4 minutes or until the chicken is cooked through.

3 Stir in the fresh Thai basil leaves. Serve the stir-fried chicken garnished with finely sliced red chillies and the deep fried Thai basil leaves, if using.

Stir-fried Turkey with Broccoli & Mushrooms

This is a really easy, tasty supper dish which works well with chicken, too.

Serves 4

INGREDIENTS
115 g/4 oz broccoli florets
4 spring onions
5 ml/1 tsp cornflour
45 ml/3 tbsp oyster sauce
15 ml/1 tbsp dark soy sauce
120 ml/4 fl oz/½ cup chicken stock
10 ml/2 tsp lemon juice
45 ml/3 tbsp groundnut oil
450 g/1 lb turkey steaks, cut into strips
    about 5 mm x 5 cm/¼ x 2 in
1 small onion, chopped
2 garlic cloves, crushed
10 ml/2 tsp grated fresh root ginger
115 g/4 oz/1½ cups shiitake
    mushrooms, sliced
75 g/3 oz baby sweetcorn, halved lengthways
15 ml/1 tbsp sesame oil
salt and freshly ground black pepper
cooked egg noodles, to serve

1 Divide the broccoli florets into smaller sprigs and cut the stalks into thin diagonal slices.

2 Finely chop the white parts of the spring onions and slice the green parts into thin shreds.

3 In a bowl, blend together the cornflour, oyster sauce, soy sauce, stock and lemon juice. Set aside.

4 Heat a wok until hot, add 30 ml/ 2 tbsp of the groundnut oil and swirl it around. Add the turkey and stir-fry for about 2 minutes until golden and crispy at the edges. Remove the turkey from the wok and keep warm.

5 Add the remaining groundnut oil to the wok and stir-fry the chopped onion, garlic and ginger over a medium heat for about 1 minute. Increase the heat to high, add the broccoli, mushrooms and sweetcorn, and stir-fry for 2 minutes.

6 Return the turkey to the wok, then add the sauce with the chopped spring onion and seasoning. Cook, stirring, for about 1 minute until the sauce has thickened. Stir in the sesame oil. Serve immediately on a bed of egg noodles with the finely shredded spring onion scattered on top.

Stir-fried Pork with Mustard

Fry the apples for this dish very carefully, because they will disintegrate if they are overcooked.

Serves 4

INGREDIENTS
500 g/1¼ lb pork fillet
1 tart apple, such as
    Granny Smith
40 g/1½ oz/3 tbsp unsalted butter
15 ml/1 tbsp caster sugar
1 small onion, finely chopped
30 ml/2 tbsp Calvados or
    other brandy
15 ml/1 tbsp Meaux or
    wholegrain mustard
150 ml/¼ pint/⅔ cup double cream
30 ml/2 tbsp chopped fresh
    flat leaf parsley
salt and freshly ground
    black pepper
fresh flat leaf parsley sprigs,
    to garnish

2 Heat a wok, then add half the butter. When the butter is hot, add the apple slices, sprinkle over the sugar and stir-fry for 2–3 minutes. Remove the apple and set aside. Wipe out the wok with kitchen paper.

3 Heat the wok again, then add the remaining butter and stir-fry the sliced pork fillet and chopped onion together for 2–3 minutes until the pork is golden and the onion has begun to soften.

1 Cut the pork fillet into thin slices. Peel and core the apple, then cut it into thick slices.

4 Stir in the Calvados or other brandy and boil until it is reduced by half. Stir in the mustard.

5 Add the cream and simmer for about 1 minute, then stir in the parsley. Season and serve garnished with sprigs of flat leaf parsley.

Glazed Lamb

Classic partners, lemon and honey, flavour this lamb stir-fry.

Serves 4

INGREDIENTS
450 g/1 lb boneless lean lamb
15 ml/1 tbsp grapeseed oil
175 g/6 oz mangetouts,
    topped and tailed
3 spring onions, sliced
30 ml/2 tbsp clear honey
juice of ½ lemon
30 ml/2 tbsp chopped fresh coriander
15 ml/1 tbsp sesame seeds
salt and freshly ground black pepper
fresh coriander sprigs, to garnish
halved lemon slices, to serve

1 Using a sharp knife, cut the lamb into thin strips. Heat a wok, then add the oil. When the oil is hot, stir-fry the lamb until browned all over. Remove from the wok and keep warm.

2 Add the mangetouts and sliced spring onions to the hot wok and stir-fry for 30 seconds. Return the lamb to the wok.

3 Add the honey, lemon juice, chopped coriander, sesame seeds and seasoning. Bring to the boil and bubble for 1 minute until the lamb is well coated in the honey mixture. Garnish with coriander sprigs and serve with the lemon slices.

Veal Escalopes with Artichokes

Canned artichoke hearts have an excellent flavour and are simple to use.

Serves 4

INGREDIENTS

450 g/1 lb veal escalopes
1 shallot
115 g/4 oz smoked bacon
400 g/14 oz can artichoke hearts in brine,
    drained and quartered
150 ml/¼ pint/⅔ cup veal stock
leaves from 3 fresh rosemary sprigs
60 ml/4 tbsp double cream
salt and freshly ground
    black pepper
sprigs of rosemary,
    to garnish

1 Using a cleaver or sharp knife, cut the veal escalopes into thin slices. Thinly slice the shallot. Finely chop the bacon.

2 Heat a wok, add the bacon and stir-fry for 2 minutes. When the fat is released, add the veal and shallot and stir-fry for 3–4 minutes.

3 Add the artichokes and stir-fry for 1 minute. Stir in the stock and rosemary leaves and simmer for 2 minutes. Add the double cream, season with salt and pepper and serve garnished with rosemary sprigs.

Sukiyaki-style Beef

This Japanese dish is a meal in itself; the recipe incorporates all the traditional elements — meat, vegetables, noodles and tofu.

Serves 4

INGREDIENTS

450 g/1 lb thick rump steak
200 g/7 oz Japanese
 rice noodles
15 ml/1 tbsp shredded suet
200 g/7 oz firm tofu
 (beancurd), cubed
8 shiitake mushrooms, trimmed
2 medium leeks, sliced into
 2.5 cm/1 in lengths
90 g/3½ oz baby spinach,
 to serve

FOR THE STOCK

15 ml/1 tbsp caster sugar
90 ml/6 tbsp Japanese rice wine
45 ml/3 tbsp dark soy sauce
120 ml/4 fl oz/½ cup water

2 To make the stock, place the sugar, rice wine, soy sauce and water in a bowl and mix well.

3 Heat a wok, then add the suet. When the suet has melted, stir-fry the beef for 2–3 minutes until it is cooked, but still pink in colour. Add the stock.

4 Add the tofu, mushrooms and leeks to the wok and cook for 4 minutes until the leeks are tender.

5 Divide the cooked vegetables, tofu and beef equally among four plates. Serve immediately, accompanied by the noodles and lightly cooked baby spinach leaves.

1 Using a sharp knife, cut the beef into thin slices. Blanch the noodles in boiling water for 2 minutes, then strain well and keep warm.

COOK'S TIP: Tofu, or beancurd, is a high-protein food made from soya beans. Its bland taste readily absorbs other flavours, and it is delicious in stir-fries. It is available from supermarkets and health food shops.

Beef Stir-fry with Crisp Parsnips

Wonderful crisp shreds of parsnip add extra crunchiness to this stir-fry, which is a great supper dish to share with friends.

Serves 4

INGREDIENTS
350 g/12 oz parsnips
450 g/1 lb rump steak
450 g/1 lb leeks
2 red peppers, seeded
350 g/12 oz courgettes
90 ml/6 tbsp vegetable oil
2 garlic cloves, crushed
45 ml/3 tbsp hoi-sin sauce
salt and freshly ground
    black pepper

1 Peel the parsnips. Cut in half lengthways, place the flat surface on the board and cut into thin strips. Finely shred each piece. Rinse in cold water and drain thoroughly. Dry on kitchen paper if necessary.

2 Cut the rump steak into thin strips. Split the leeks in half lengthways and thickly slice at an angle. Roughly chop the red peppers and thinly slice the courgettes.

3 Heat the oil in a wok. Fry the parsnips until crisp and golden. You may need to do this in batches, adding a little more oil if necessary. Remove with a slotted spoon and drain on kitchen paper.

4 Keep the crisply fried parsnips warm while you prepare the steak. Stir-fry the steak in the wok until golden and cooked through. You may need to do this in batches, adding more oil if necessary. Remove and drain on kitchen paper.

5 Stir-fry the garlic, leeks, peppers and courgettes for about 10 minutes or until golden brown and beginning to soften but still retaining a little bite. Season the mixture well.

6 Return the meat to the pan with the hoi-sin sauce. Stir-fry for 2–3 minutes or until piping hot. Adjust the seasoning and serve with the crisply fried parsnips piled on top.

Stir-fried Chick-peas

Lightly spiced chick-peas are combined with tomatoes and spinach and topped with toasted sunflower seeds.

Serves 2–4 as an accompaniment

INGREDIENTS
30 ml/2 tbsp sunflower seeds
400 g/14 oz can chick-peas,
 drained and rinsed
5 ml/1 tsp chilli powder
5 ml/1 tsp paprika
30 ml/2 tbsp vegetable oil
1 garlic clove, crushed
200 g/7 oz canned chopped tomatoes
225 g/8 oz spinach, coarse
 stalks removed
salt and freshly ground black pepper
10 ml/2 tsp chilli oil

1 Heat a wok, add the sunflower seeds and dry fry until golden. Remove from the wok and set aside. Toss the chick-peas in the chilli powder and paprika; remove and reserve.

2 Reheat the wok, then add the oil. When the oil is hot, stir-fry the garlic for 30 seconds. Add the chick-peas and stir-fry for 1 minute.

3 Stir in the tomatoes and stir-fry for 4 minutes. Toss in the spinach, season well and stir-fry for 1 minute. Drizzle the chilli oil and scatter the sunflower seeds over the vegetables, then serve.

Spiced Tofu Stir-fry

Serves 4

INGREDIENTS

225 g/8 oz/generous 3 cups
    brown-cap mushrooms
1 bunch spring onions
10 ml/2 tsp ground cumin
15 ml/1 tbsp paprika
5 ml/1 tsp ground ginger
good pinch of cayenne pepper
15 ml/1 tbsp caster sugar
275 g/10 oz firm tofu (beancurd), cubed
60 ml/4 tbsp oil
2 garlic cloves, crushed
1 red pepper, seeded and sliced
1 yellow pepper, seeded and sliced
1 large courgette, sliced
115 g/4 oz fine green beans, halved
50 g/2 oz/scant ½ cup pine nuts
15 ml/1 tbsp lime juice
15 ml/1 tbsp clear honey
salt and freshly ground black pepper

1 Halve or quarter the mushrooms, if large. Cut the spring onions into 2 cm/¾ in lengths.

2 Mix together the spices, sugar and seasoning. Add the tofu and toss to coat. Heat some oil in a wok and cook the tofu over a high heat for 3–4 minutes, turning occasionally. Remove with a slotted spoon. Wipe out the pan with kitchen paper.

3 Add a little more oil to the pan and cook the garlic and spring onions for 3 minutes. Add the remaining vegetables and cook over a medium heat for 6 minutes or until beginning to soften and turn golden. Season well.

4 Return the tofu to the pan with the pine nuts, lime juice and honey. Heat through and serve immediately.

Stir-fried Vegetables with Coriander Omelette

This is a great supper dish for vegetarians. The glaze is added here only to make the mixture shine; it is not intended as a sauce.

Serves 3–4

INGREDIENTS

2 eggs
30 ml/2 tbsp water
45 ml/3 tbsp chopped fresh coriander
salt and freshly ground black pepper
45 ml/3 tbsp groundnut oil
5 ml/1 tsp grated fresh root ginger
6–8 spring onions, sliced
115 g/4 oz mangetouts
1 yellow pepper, seeded and sliced
115 g/4 oz shiitake or button mushrooms
75 g/3 oz (drained weight) canned water
   chestnuts, rinsed
115 g/4 oz/½ cup beansprouts
½ small Chinese cabbage, coarsely shredded

FOR THE GLAZE
15 ml/1 tbsp cornflour
30 ml/2 tbsp dry sherry
30 ml/2 tbsp soy sauce
15 ml/1 tbsp sweet chilli sauce
120 ml/4 fl oz/½ cup vegetable stock

1 To make the omelette, whisk the eggs, water, coriander and seasoning in a small bowl. Heat 15 ml/1 tbsp of the oil in a wok. Pour in the eggs, then tilt the wok so that the mixture spreads to an even layer. Cook over a high heat until the edges are slightly crisp.

2 With a spatula or palette knife, flip the omelette over and cook the other side for about 30 seconds until lightly browned. Turn the omelette on to a board and leave to cool. Roll up loosely and cut into thin slices. Wipe out the wok with kitchen paper.

3 To make the glaze, blend together the cornflour, sherry, soy sauce, chilli sauce and stock in a bowl. Set aside.

4 Reheat the wok until hot, add the oil and swirl it around. Add the ginger and spring onions and stir-fry for a few seconds to flavour the oil. Add the mangetouts, yellow pepper, mushrooms and the water chestnuts and stir-fry for 3 minutes.

VARIATION: Vary the combination of vegetables used according to availability and taste.

5 Add the beansprouts and Chinese cabbage and stir-fry for 2 minutes. Pour in the glaze and cook, stirring, for about 1 minute until the mixture thickens and coats the vegetables.

6 Turn the vegetables on to a warmed serving plate and top with the omelette slices. Serve at once.

Black Bean & Vegetable Stir-fry

This colourful mixture of spring onions, mushrooms, red and green peppers, carrots and beansprouts is coated in a classic Chinese sauce.

Serves 4

INGREDIENTS
8 spring onions
225 g/8 oz/3 cups button mushrooms
1 red pepper
1 green pepper
2 large carrots
60 ml/4 tbsp sesame oil
2 garlic cloves, crushed
60 ml/4 tbsp black bean sauce
90 ml/6 tbsp warm water
225 g/8 oz/1 cup beansprouts
salt and freshly ground black pepper

3 Heat the sesame oil in a wok until very hot. Add the sliced spring onions and crushed garlic and stir-fry for 30 seconds.

1 Thinly slice the spring onions and button mushrooms. Cut both the peppers in half, remove the seeds and slice the flesh into thin strips.

2 Cut the carrots in half, then cut each half into thin strips lengthways. Stack the slices and cut through them to make very fine strips.

4 Add the mushrooms, peppers and carrots. Stir-fry for 5–6 minutes over a high heat until the vegetables are just beginning to soften.

COOK'S TIP: For best results the oil in the wok must be very hot before the vegetables are added so that they remain crunchy.

5 In a bowl, mix the black bean sauce with the water. Add to the wok and cook for 3–4 minutes.

6 Stir in the beansprouts and stir-fry for 1 minute more until all the vegetables are coated in the sauce. Season with salt and pepper to taste. Serve at once.

Spring Vegetable Stir-fry

This dish is delicious served with marinated tofu and noodles.

Serves 4

INGREDIENTS
15 ml/1 tbsp groundnut or vegetable oil
5 ml/1 tsp sesame oil
1 garlic clove, chopped
2.5 cm/1 in piece fresh root ginger, peeled
    and finely chopped
225 g/8 oz baby carrots
350 g/12 oz broccoli florets
175 g/6 oz asparagus tips
2 spring onions, sliced on the diagonal
175 g/6 oz spring greens,
    finely shredded
30 ml/2 tbsp light soy sauce
15 ml/1 tbsp apple juice
15 ml/1 tbsp sesame seeds, toasted

1 Heat a wok over a high heat. Add the oils, then reduce the heat. Add the garlic and sauté for 1 minute.

2 Add the next four ingredients and stir-fry for 4 minutes. Add the spring onions and spring greens and stir-fry for a further 2 minutes.

3 Add the soy sauce and apple juice and cook for 1–2 minutes; add a little water if necessary. Sprinkle with sesame seeds and serve.

Oriental Green Beans

A tasty way of enlivening green beans; delicious hot or cold.

Serves 4

INGREDIENTS
450 g/1 lb green beans
15 ml/1 tbsp olive oil
5 ml/1 tsp sesame oil
2 garlic cloves, crushed
2.5 cm/1 in piece fresh root ginger, peeled
    and finely chopped
30 ml/2 tbsp dark
    soy sauce

1 Steam the beans over a saucepan of boiling salted water for 6 minutes or until just tender.

2 Meanwhile, heat the olive and sesame oils in a wok, add the garlic and sauté for 1 minute.

3 Stir in the ginger and soy sauce and cook, stirring constantly, for a further 2–3 minutes until the liquid has reduced, then pour this mixture over the warm beans. Leave for a few minutes to allow all the flavours to mingle before serving.

Right: Spring Vegetable Stir-fry (top); Oriental Green Beans

Mooli, Beetroot & Carrot Stir-fry

This is a dazzlingly colourful and fragrant dish with a crunchy texture.

Serves 4 as an accompaniment

INGREDIENTS
25 g/1 oz/¼ cup pine nuts
115 g/4 oz mooli, peeled
115 g/4 oz raw beetroot, peeled
115 g/4 oz carrots, peeled
25 ml/1½ tbsp vegetable oil
juice of 1 orange
30 ml/2 tbsp chopped fresh coriander
salt and freshly ground black pepper

1 Heat a wok, then add the pine nuts and toss until golden brown. Remove and set aside. Cut the mooli, beetroot and carrots into long, thin strips.

2 Reheat the wok and add one-third of the oil. When the oil is hot, stir-fry the mooli for 2–3 minutes. Remove and set aside. Cook the beetroot and carrots in separate batches in the same way.

3 Pour the orange juice into the wok and simmer for 2 minutes. Remove and keep warm.

4 Arrange the vegetables in bundles in the wok, and sprinkle over the coriander and seasoning. Drizzle over the orange juice, sprinkle in the pine nuts and serve, arranging the vegetables attractively.

Stir-fried Mixed Vegetables

It is worth frying the sesame seeds: they add an extra dimension.

Serves 4

INGREDIENTS
40 ml/2½ tbsp groundnut oil
25 ml/1½ tbsp sesame seeds
2 carrots, cut into matchsticks
115 g/4 oz French beans,
    blanched for 2 minutes
    and refreshed
6 shiitake mushrooms,
    stalks removed and caps
    thinly sliced
2 thin yellow or green courgettes,
    cut into matchsticks
15 ml/1 tbsp soy sauce
few drops of
    sesame oil

1 Heat a wok and add 10 ml/2 tsp of the oil. Add the sesame seeds and cook, stirring and shaking the wok, for 1 minute or until golden. Turn the seeds on to kitchen paper to drain.

2 Reheat the wok and add the remaining oil. Add the carrots and stir-fry for 2 minutes. Add the French beans and mushrooms. Stir-fry for 1 minute. Add the courgettes and stir-fry for 2–3 minutes or until all the vegetables are just tender.

3 Add the soy sauce and sesame oil with the sesame seeds. Toss well and serve immediately.

Special Fried Rice

This tasty dish is excellent for using up small quantities of leftovers.
It makes an ideal light lunch or supper.

Serves 4

INGREDIENTS
50 g/2 oz cooked peeled prawns
3 eggs
5 ml/1 tsp salt
3 spring onions, finely chopped
60 ml/4 tbsp vegetable oil
115 g/4 oz/1 cup peas
50 g/2 oz/⅓ cup cooked ham, finely diced
15 ml/1 tbsp light soy sauce
15 ml/1 tbsp Chinese rice wine or dry sherry
450 g/1 lb cooked rice

1 Pat dry the prawns with kitchen paper. In a bowl, lightly beat the eggs with a pinch of the salt and a few pieces of the spring onions.

2 Heat a wok and add about half of the vegetable oil. Add the peas, prawns and ham and stir-fry for 1 minute, then add the soy sauce and wine or sherry. Remove from the wok and keep warm.

3 Heat the remaining oil in the wok and lightly scramble the eggs. Add the rice and stir to make sure that each grain is separated.

4 Add the remaining salt, the prawns, ham and peas and two-thirds of the remaining spring onions. Blend the rice and vegetables well and serve either hot or cold, garnished with the rest of the spring onions.

Chinese Jewelled Rice

A glorious rice dish with many different, interesting ingredients and flavours. A mouthwatering meal in itself.

Serves 4

INGREDIENTS
350 g/12 oz/1¾ cups long grain rice
45 ml/3 tbsp vegetable oil
1 onion, roughly chopped
115 g/4 oz/⅔ cup cooked ham, diced
175 g/6 oz canned white
  crab meat
75 g/3 oz canned water chestnuts,
  drained and sliced
4 dried black Chinese mushrooms, soaked,
  drained and diced
115 g/4 oz/1 cup peas
30 ml/2 tbsp oyster sauce
5 ml/1 tsp sugar
Chinese chives, to garnish

1 Rinse the long grain rice, then cook for 10–12 minutes in 750–900 ml/1¼–1½ pints/3–3¾ cups water in a saucepan with a tight-fitting lid. Refresh under cold water. Heat a wok, add half the oil and stir-fry the rice for 3 minutes, then remove and set aside.

2 Add the remaining oil to the wok. When the oil is hot, cook the onion until softened but not coloured. Add all the remaining ingredients and stir-fry for 2 minutes.

3 Return the rice to the wok and stir-fry for 3 minutes. Garnish with Chinese chives and serve immediately.

Indonesian Pork & Prawn Rice

Rice is the main ingredient of this famous Indonesian dish, known as *Nasi Goreng*, although almost anything can be added for colour and flavour. A rich flavour is provided by chillies and authentic sauces.

Serves 4–6

INGREDIENTS

3 eggs
60 ml/4 tbsp vegetable oil
6 shallots or 1 large
  onion, chopped
2 garlic cloves, crushed
2.5 cm/1 in piece fresh root ginger,
  peeled and chopped
2–3 small fresh red chillies, seeded and
  finely chopped
15 ml/1 tbsp tamarind sauce
1 cm/½ in cube shrimp paste or
  15 ml/1 tbsp fish sauce
2.5 ml/½ tsp ground turmeric
30 ml/2 tbsp creamed coconut
juice of 2 limes
10 ml/2 tsp sugar
350 g/12 oz lean pork or chicken breast
  fillets, skinned and sliced
350 g/12 oz fresh or cooked prawns,
  peeled but tails intact
175 g/6 oz/¾ cup beansprouts
175 g/6 oz Chinese leaves, shredded
175 g/6 oz/1½ cups frozen
  peas, thawed
250 g/9 oz/1¼ cups long grain rice,
  cooked to make 675 g/1½ lb
salt
1 small bunch fresh coriander or basil,
  roughly chopped, to garnish

1 In a bowl, beat the eggs with a pinch of salt. Heat a wok over a moderate heat. Pour in the eggs and move the pan around until they begin to set. When set, remove from the wok, roll up and slice thinly. Cover and set aside.

2 Wipe the wok clean with kitchen paper. Heat 15 ml/1 tbsp of the oil in the wok and fry the shallots or onion until evenly brown. Remove from the wok, set aside and keep warm.

3 Heat the remaining oil in the wok, add the garlic, ginger and chillies and soften without colouring. Stir in the tamarind and shrimp paste or fish sauce, turmeric, coconut, lime juice, sugar and 2.5 ml/½ tsp salt. Combine briefly over a moderate heat. Add the pork or chicken and prawns and fry for 3–4 minutes.

4 Add the beansprouts, Chinese leaves and peas and cook briefly. Add the rice and stir-fry for 6–8 minutes, stirring to prevent it from burning.

5 Turn out on to a large serving plate, decorate with sliced egg pancake, the fried shallots or onion and chopped coriander or basil. Serve immediately.

Fried Rice with Mushrooms

This uncomplicated dish will be a great favourite with vegetarians and meat-eaters alike. Sesame oil adds a subtle nutty flavour to the rice.

Serves 4

INGREDIENTS

225 g/8 oz/generous 1 cup
   long grain rice
15 ml/1 tbsp vegetable oil
1 egg, lightly beaten
2 garlic cloves, crushed
175 g/6 oz/2½ cups button
   mushrooms, sliced
15 ml/1 tbsp light
   soy sauce
1.5 ml/¼ tsp salt
2.5 ml/½ tsp sesame oil
cucumber matchsticks,
   to garnish

1 Rinse the rice until the water runs clear, then drain thoroughly. Place it in a saucepan and just cover with cold water.

2 Bring the water to the boil. Stir, boil for a few minutes, then cover the pan. Lower the heat to a simmer and cook the rice gently for 5–8 minutes until all the water has been absorbed.

3 Remove the pan from the heat and, without lifting the lid, leave for another 10 minutes before stirring or forking up the rice so that it is completely cooked.

4 Heat 5 ml/1 tsp of the vegetable oil in a non-stick wok. Add the egg and cook, stirring with chopsticks or a wooden spoon, until scrambled. Remove from the wok and set aside.

5 Heat the remaining vegetable oil in the wok. Stir-fry the garlic for a few seconds, then add the mushrooms and stir-fry for 2 minutes, adding a little water, if needed, to prevent burning.

6 Stir in the cooked rice and cook for about 4 minutes or until the rice is hot, stirring from time to time.

7 Add the scrambled egg, light soy sauce, salt and sesame oil. Cook for 1 minute to heat through. Serve the fried rice immediately, garnished with cucumber matchsticks.

Noodles with Ginger & Coriander

Here is a simple noodle stir-fry that goes well with most oriental dishes.

Serves 4–6

INGREDIENTS
handful of fresh coriander sprigs
225 g/8 oz dried egg noodles
45 ml/3 tbsp groundnut oil
5 cm/2 in piece fresh root ginger, peeled and
    cut into fine shreds
6–8 spring onions, cut into shreds
30 ml/2 tbsp light soy sauce
salt and freshly ground black pepper

1 Strip the leaves from the coriander stalks. Pile them on a chopping board and coarsely chop them using a cleaver or large, sharp knife.

2 Cook the noodles in boiling water according to the packet instructions. Rinse under cold water and drain well. Toss in 15 ml/1 tbsp of the groundnut oil.

3 Heat a wok until hot, add the remaining oil and swirl it around. Add the ginger and stir-fry for a few seconds, then add the noodles and spring onions. Stir-fry for 3–4 minutes until hot.

4 Sprinkle over the soy sauce, coriander and seasoning. Toss well, then serve at once.

Singapore Rice Vermicelli

This lightly curried rice noodle dish is simple and speedily prepared.

Serves 4

INGREDIENTS

225 g/8 oz/2 cups dried rice vermicelli
15 ml/1 tbsp vegetable oil
1 egg, lightly beaten
2 garlic cloves, finely chopped
1 large fresh red or green chilli, seeded and finely chopped
15 ml/1 tbsp medium curry powder
1 red pepper, seeded and thinly sliced
1 green pepper, seeded and thinly sliced
1 carrot, cut into matchsticks
1.5 ml/¼ tsp salt
60 ml/4 tbsp vegetable stock
115 g/4 oz cooked peeled prawns, thawed if frozen
75 g/3 oz/½ cup lean ham, cut into 1 cm/½ in cubes
15 ml/1 tbsp light soy sauce

1 Soak the rice vermicelli in a bowl of boiling water for 4 minutes, or according to the packet instructions, then drain thoroughly and set aside.

2 Heat 5 ml/1 tsp of the oil in a non-stick wok. Add the egg and scramble until set. Remove with a slotted spoon and set aside.

3 Heat the remaining oil in the clean pan. Stir-fry the garlic and chilli for a few seconds, then stir in the curry powder. Cook for 1 minute, stirring, then add the next five ingredients.

4 Bring to the boil. Mix in the prawns, ham, egg, vermicelli and soy sauce. Cook, stirring until all the liquid is absorbed and the mixture hot. Serve.

Rice Noodles with Beef & Black Bean Sauce

This is an excellent combination – beef with a chilli sauce tossed with silky-smooth rice noodles.

Serves 4

INGREDIENTS
450 g/1 lb fresh rice noodles
60 ml/4 tbsp vegetable oil
1 onion, finely sliced
2 garlic cloves, finely chopped
2 slices fresh root ginger, peeled and
    finely chopped
225 g/8 oz mixed peppers, seeded and
    cut into strips
350 g/12 oz rump steak, finely sliced
    against the grain
45 ml/3 tbsp fermented black beans,
    rinsed in warm water,
    drained and chopped
30 ml/2 tbsp soy sauce
30 ml/2 tbsp oyster sauce
15 ml/1 tbsp chilli black bean sauce
15 ml/1 tbsp cornflour
120 ml/4 fl oz/½ cup stock or water
salt and freshly ground black pepper
2 spring onions, finely chopped,
    and 2 fresh red chillies, seeded and
    finely sliced, to garnish

1 Rinse the noodles in hot water; drain well. Heat half the oil in a wok, swirling it around. Add the onion, garlic, ginger and mixed pepper strips. Stir-fry the vegetables for 3–5 minutes, then remove with a slotted spoon and keep hot.

2 Add the remaining oil to the wok. When it is hot, add the sliced beef and fermented black beans and stir-fry over a high heat for 5 minutes or until the meat is cooked.

3 In a small bowl, blend the soy sauce, oyster sauce and chilli black bean sauce with the cornflour and stock or water until smooth.

4 Add the sauce mixture to the wok, then return the onion mixture to the wok and cook, for 1 minute, stirring continuously.

5 Add the noodles and mix lightly. Stir over a medium heat until the noodles are heated through. Adjust the seasoning if necessary. Serve at once, garnished with the chopped spring onions and chillies.

Tomato Noodles

Serves 4

INGREDIENTS
350 g/12 oz medium-thick dried egg noodles
60 ml/4 tbsp vegetable oil
2 garlic cloves, very finely chopped
4 shallots, chopped
2.5 ml/½ tsp chilli powder
5 ml/1 tsp paprika
2 carrots, finely diced
115 g/4 oz/1½ cups button
   mushrooms, quartered
50 g/2 oz/½ cup peas
15 ml/1 tbsp tomato ketchup
10 ml/2 tsp tomato purée
butter, for frying
4 quail's eggs
salt and freshly ground
   black pepper

1 Cook the noodles in boiling water according to the packet instructions. Drain, rinse again and drain well.

2 Heat the oil in a wok. Add the next four ingredients. Stir-fry for about 1 minute. Add the vegetables and stir-fry until they are cooked. Stir in the tomato ketchup and purée. Add the noodles and cook until heated through. Season.

3 Melt the butter in a frying pan and fry the eggs. Season the noodle mixture, divide it among four serving plates and top each with a fried egg.

Curry Fried Noodles

Serves 4

INGREDIENTS
60 ml/4 tbsp vegetable oil
30–45 ml/2–3 tbsp curry paste
225 g/8 oz smoked tofu (beancurd),
   cut into 2.5 cm/1 in cubes
225 g/8 oz green beans, cut into
   2.5 cm/1 in lengths
1 red pepper, seeded and cut into fine strips
350 g/12 oz/3 cups rice noodles,
   soaked in hot water until soft
15 ml/1 tbsp soy sauce
salt and freshly ground black pepper
2 spring onions, finely sliced, 2 fresh red
   chillies, seeded and chopped, and 1 lime,
   cut into wedges, to garnish

1 Heat half the oil in a wok or large frying pan. Add the curry paste and stir-fry for a few minutes, then add the tofu and fry until golden brown. Remove the tofu from the pan and set aside.

2 Add the remaining oil to the wok. When hot, add the beans and pepper. Stir-fry until cooked. Drain the noodles, add them to the wok and stir-fry until heated through.

3 Return the tofu to the wok. Add soy sauce and seasoning. Garnish with spring onions, chillies and lime wedges. Serve.

Right: Tomato Noodles (top);
Curry Fried Noodles

This edition is published by Southwater

Distributed in the UK by
The Manning Partnership,
251–253 London Road East, Batheaston,
Bath BA1 7RL, UK
tel. (0044) 01225 852 727
fax. (0044) 01225 852 852

Distributed in Australia by
Sandstone Publishing,
Unit 1, 360 Norton Street, Leichhardt,
New South Wales 2040, Australia
tel. (0061) 2 9560 7888
fax. (0061) 2 9560 7488

Distributed in New Zealand by
Five Mile Press NZ,
PO Box 33–1071, Takapuna,
Auckland 9, New Zealand
tel. (0064) 9 4444 144
fax. (0064) 9 4444 518

Southwater is an imprint of Anness Publishing Limited

© 2000 Anness Publishing Limited

Publisher: Joanna Lorenz
Editor: Valerie Ferguson
Series Designer: Bobbie Colgate Stone
Designer: Andrew Heath
Editorial Reader: Marion Wilson
Production Controller: Joanna King

Recipes contributed by: Kit Chan,
Matthew Drennan, Sarah Edmonds, Shirley Gill,
Nicola Graimes, Deh-Ta Hsuing, Norma MacMillan,
Kathy Man, Liz Trigg, Steven Wheeler.

Photography: William Adams-Lingwood,
Edward Allwright, James Duncan, Michelle Garrett,
Amanda Heywood, Thomas Odulate.

1 3 5 7 9 10 8 6 4 2

Notes:
For all recipes, quantities are given in both metric and imperial measures and, where appropriate, measures are also given in standard cups and spoons.
Follow one set, but not a mixture, because they are not interchangeable.

Standard spoon and cup measures are level.

1 tsp = 5 ml   1 tbsp = 15 ml

1 cup = 250 ml/8 fl oz

Australian standard tablespoons are 20 ml.
Australian readers should use 3 tsp in place of 1 tbsp for measuring small quantities of gelatine, cornflour, salt, etc.

Medium eggs are used unless otherwise stated.